How to Design Your Own Clothes

by

HANNAH CORBETT SHELTON

INTRODUCTION BY
IRVIN S. COBB

INFORMAL SKETCHES BY THE AUTHOR

1934
NEW YORK
LEISURE LEAGUE OF AMERICA

PRINTED AND BOUND IN
THE UNITED STATES OF AMERICA
BY
THE MAPLE PRESS CO.

CONTENTS

FOREWORD

I SUPPOSE I know as much—which means as little—about the fashioning of feminine garments as the average man does. Being, I trust, an average man I know when a woman seems to be smartly dressed and becomingly turned out. I get that sense of subtle affinity between the clothes and the wearer which we call good taste, but exactly what preliminary steps have been taken to achieve that exceedingly worthwhile result, remain, so far as I am concerned, profound mysteries. I admire the finished product; perhaps, dimly, I wonder what might have been the processes by which the accomplishment was brought about, but for me that, substantially, is all. So for me to be trying to write an introduction for a book of this type is mildly humorous to start with.

My excuse for writing it is that I know the author of it, and tremendously admire her on her own account, and because of the notable success she has achieved in her chosen field. I have known her since her childhood. She began her professional career, as I may testify from reliable hearsay evidence, with a certain natural ability; to that ability she added perseverance, gallantry, determination, enthusiasm. Through hard knocks and long experience, she learned her calling so well that I am very sure she must abundantly be qualified to teach it to others.

In any event her daily life has been an example in pluck and cheerfulness and earnest endeavor to everyone about her. Moreover she has that precious thing—a true sense of humor—which means the ability to laugh at herself with the same gaiety of spirit with which she laughs at the rest of the world.

Perhaps she weaves the essences of these qualities into the wares she designs. On second thought I am sure she must do this very thing. Unless she did it, she wouldn't be the Hannah Corbett Shelton I know.

Irvin S. Cobb

RAVELINGS FROM THE WORKSHOP OF A DESIGNER

I'D LIKE to make a little wager with every woman who reads these pages that at some time or other she has experienced a very real desire either to make or to design a dress for herself. Something has told her that with this, that, or the other costume she could be more charming, more attractive, could "land" that man or this job. In other words, if you are sure your clothes are right you are armored for any fray – 99 per cent of the battle is won.

Not all of us are born with creative ability (though there is far more of it in us than most of us realize), but we do have good sense, and we can learn designing just as we learned arithmetic, geography, or history. I do not believe any art gives a wider range for self-expression than dress designing. According to your ability and practice, you can plan a simple or an elaborate costume. Every possible color is yours for the using; tailor-made lines or the graceful lines of the draped costume, a matter of personal choice and becoming-ness; the quality of your material cheap and effective, or expensive and enduring, as you wish or as your purse dictates.

9

HOW TO DESIGN YOUR OWN CLOTHES

Design your own clothes! Make a dress! If either sounds like a large order, you are wrong. If you so desire you can acquire the art of making your clothes but if for some good reason you haven't time to sew you may at least sketch and explain your ideas to a seamstress who can carry them out.

Aside from being useful, gratifying, and perhaps economical, designing has still another value. Every garment you make is an expression of your inventiveness, your ingenuity, your creativeness. The intriguing stories of how dresses grow from ideas to finished products would fill volumes. One woman sees a lovely neckline, a neckline she knows would flatter her. Then and there the idea for a new dress begins to take form. Another woman sees a piece of material she must have, regardless of cost, because it is her favorite color, or because it has a gorgeous texture; in other words, because for some reason it just suits her. Another has an old piece of jewelry which demands the proper dress as a setting.

Nature—flowers, birds, trees—gives us countless color ideas. Men's clothes have suggested a number of styles in women's wear. The bell hop's coat, the mess jacket, the simple pique vest are examples. Ideas for women's clothes are garnered from everywhere and nowhere. If something inspirational in that line is stirring in your head why not work it out in cloth and enjoy the fun of telling your

10

friends that the frock they are admiring is of your own design and making? In my years of experience in designing for the wholesake market, creative ideas have come to me from varied sources. I recall some years ago being tired and depressed and feeling that I should have a rest. Five days later found me at White Sulphur Springs, Virginia, my one object to forget everything pertaining to clothes. When the train pulled into the station and the porter assisted me outside I began to relax and to decide what I most wanted to do. Horseback riding had once been my hobby so I decided to get into riding habit as soon as possible.

The bridle paths leading up the mountains were so very steep and narrow we rode single file. The divine quietness of the place with its exquisite scenery was unbelievable. Scarcely a twig moved; the birds sang softly; the clouds hung almost within reach. The flower-covered mountain was a mass of color—wild-violet blue, daisy yellow, fern green. How could I resist dismounting and filling my arms with flowers, purple and yellow. What a combination! And suddenly it became a dress! Orchid chiffon embroidered in tiny yellow daisies, long flowing sleeves, plain tight bodice, sash of deep purple velvet. A blonde, a brunette, even a red head would be gorgeous in such a dress! Or Mother with her lovely gray hair! I fairly shouted my delight!

"Is yer goin' to the top of the mountain, Miss, or ain't yer?" the groom wanted to know, no doubt considering me fairly out of my mind.

Some time later a trip to Paris promised a five-day rest. I determined to think of nothing but pleasure until the boat landed, and I became obliged to concentrate on Parisian models and what I would do with them on my return to New York. Two days out, while standing at the bow of the *Ile de France*, I became fascinated with the waves. How they changed color as they crashed against the boat and receded! Aquamarine, black recesses, the whole tipped with sea-blue green and foamy white. A dress possibility which I couldn't let escape! And no sooner had it begun formulating in my tired brain, than I raised my eyes to watch the sun sink slowly behind a cloud. What colors here! More beauty to be interpreted in terms of feminine apparel! And so it goes. Once conscious of a desire to create, try as you may, you cannot escape it!

Designing does not mean that you are to dig down in your brain and think up every detail of your dress. The complete idea is more likely to be assembled after this fashion: you are looking through a style magazine, you see a new sleeve which interests you, but neither neckline or skirt is to your liking. You look further and find neck-line and other details which you do want. Putting these together spells designing. Again, you may have a definite idea in mind which you haven't seen anywhere. When such an idea suggests itself don't be afraid to use it. Work it out in inexpensive material, but do try it. This is creative ability and should be cultivated. Many a woman in trying to utilize a remnant has created a garment which has far surpassed in design, beauty, and usefulness any style she may have found in a fashion book.

A few instances come to mind of the origin of some of my own creations. Some years ago, I remember admiring a cretonne pattern in which the figure of a parrot was predominant. For several days I was haunted by an image of the parrot. I bought a piece of the cretonne, cut out the pattern, and toyed with it. Finally I decided to embroider my parrot on the pocket of a dress, which necessitated, of course, a dress to harmonize with the pocket! The effect was striking and most successful. Again, while engaged in a game of bridge, the futuristic pattern on a deck of cards gave me another idea for a motif.

I hope I'm not betraying any secrets of my trade when I say that sometimes a good dress is the result of an accident. I remember designing a one-piece dress of which the skirt was cut wrong, obliging me to make a new one, since the original bolt of material was exhausted. I found, while working on the new material, that I could convert

13

the dress on the spur of the moment into a two-piece affair, giving an effect far more interesting than the original design. Once I created a dress with a mustard top and brown skirt which I could not complete until more material was ordered. I hung the dress on the rack and proceeded with something else on hand when my eye fell on a heap of brown and mustard scraps accidentally arranged in interesting angles. I picked them up and worked them into a scarf by imitating the casual order I had observed which was exactly the effect my incomplete dress needed.

Necklines, and accessories in general, are so important that I am particularly observant of them on any dress I see, no matter where. In the designing of a dress the neckline is the first step I consider and I must confess I am often completely stuck for a new idea. The other day I heard of another designer who probably felt in the same desperate mood. Her pet trick is to make a group of dresses without deciding on necklines. Not long ago she had several dresses complete but for collars and neck finishings. So out she went scouting. She covered Madison Avenue and part of Fifty-seventh Street without success. But when she turned into Fifth Avenue she saw a beautifully dressed woman leaving one of the smarter shops and wearing a neckline which the designer was instantly sure of wanting. But before she could see it well, the woman

14

had been swallowed up by a taxi. Losing no time the designer plunged into the next taxi to trail the woman whose gown she must see. They dodged through traffic, sped on and on. At last the pursued taxi stopped, the two passengers tumbled out on the sidewalk, the designer just in time to see the woman with the intriguing neckline throw her fur scarf across her shoulder and sail into a hotel. I have yet to endanger my life with a wild taxi ride but I certainly shouldn't hesitate if the idea were worth going after.

You will be interested, I'm sure, in the story of the Irvin S. Cobb smock. "By the way," Mr. Cobb remarked to me one day, "would you like to listen to the story of my latest creation?" Delighted, I settled myself in his lazy studio chair to hear of his new brain child, which, to my very great surprise, proved not to be a story, a book, or a joke, but a smock designed entirely by himself! Necessity, it seemed, had prompted this outburst of talent.

For many years before the war, he told me, while writing or dictating to his secretary, he had been a slave to the habit of twisting buttons off of his coat and vest. He decided he would have to do something about it. Having spent a great deal of time in various countries of Europe as war correspondent for several of New York's largest newspapers, he had seen children, and laborers

as well, wearing garments resembling the artist's
smock, usually made of dark blue but buttoned in
the back. This, felt Mr. Cobb, would prove his
great "button saver"! He went to his shirtmaker
and made a rough pencil sketch of his idea. The
result was practical, delightful, and certainly served
its purpose. A straight affair it was, reaching to
the knees, with a yoke and four large pearl buttons
at the back, the collar much like a man's shirt
collar. Two front patch pockets were "catchalls"
for cigars, pencils, handkerchiefs, and the like.
A flowing necktie and leather belt (and for Mr.
Irvin Cobb's merry girth, "some" belt) completed
the smock.

Immediately I saw the possibilities for artists,
writers, architects, and also girl stenographers,
models, housewives, or laboratory technicians. Mr.
Cobb offered to let me make the smock and to use
his name if I wished to put it on the market. Gaily
he sketched his monogram for the label, and six
weeks later Lord and Taylor of New York City
was featuring the I.S.C. smock with but a slight
change from the original; changed only enough
to adapt it to women's as well as men's use. On
page 17 are sketches of the original smock (A) and
my adaptation (B). Golf and tennis players have
liked it. The wife who drives her husband to the
station in the suburb uses it as a housedress, for
it looks like a sports costume. It makes a perfect

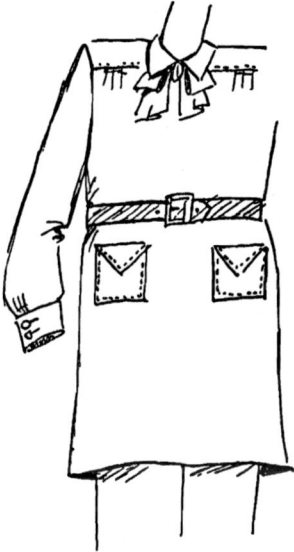

(A)

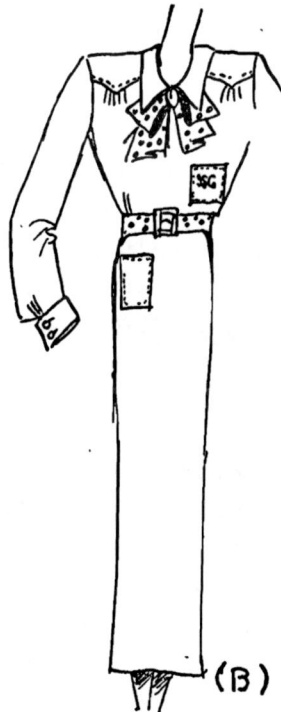

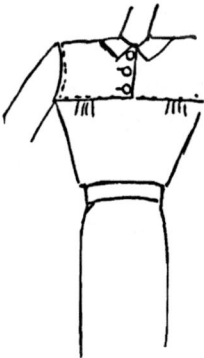

(B)

IRVIN S. COBB SMOCK AND AN ADAPTATION

17

overall garment for the woman gardener. Men and women students wear it for "lab" work, liking it for its combination of complete protection and smart appearance.

The designing of clothes is really so simple. Pick a becoming color, becoming lines, concentrate on the finishing touches, and you have designed quite by yourself something with that original and personal note; a little trick within the ability of even a fifteen-year-old girl.

And speaking of the teen-age girl, look out ahead, mothers! Here's a sermon to you who discourage your young daughter who wants to try making her own clothes. It's far more economical for her to waste a few yards of material now, with your interest and encouragement, than to start her out in life knowing nothing about sewing. There is no better way to teach your little or big girl to care for her clothes and take an interest in wearing them correctly than by encouraging her interest in making them. I personally began learning to design at the age of five when I made doll clothes, every original pattern of which brought forth the appreciation and interest of the entire household.

I am asked by the beginner: What is the first thing to do in designing a dress? My answer is: There is no rule for design, but rather, a definite plan for making the garment. It might surprise you to know that designing and sewing in the largest and most exclusive dressmaking establishment in New York City is little different from what goes on in the home where the dining-room table furnishes the cutting board.

Would a picture of my workroom on the eighteenth floor of a New York skyscraper interest you? The portrait of myself, the designer, drawn by my friends who have never seen me at work is amusing. They see me arrayed in a stunning gown sitting apart, intent on the capturing of that nebulous thing, an idea. On the contrary, I am merely the captain of a busy crew figuratively in shirt-sleeves and on my feet most of the day. With me are four girls and two tailors. At one time or another I supervise each and constantly keep my eye on them all, for I must follow the development of a dress from beginning to end. Belts, boxes of buttons, yards of material, ironing boards, dummies, and a sewing-machine are within reach, for the garment which has been sketched must actually be worked out to the last buttonhole before we are ready to show it to the buyer.

The paraphernalia is, after all, the same as that which your own sewing room requires, and at the end of a day my workroom but a replica of yours—a jumble of everything we have had in our hands! But—on the model there is a perfect-fitting, "ready-to-wear," and oftentimes entrancingly beautiful gown.

19

SKETCHING YOUR OWN DRESS

YEARS ago I was told that to be able to sketch a dress, I must, by years of hard work sketching from the nude, learn the lines of the body. If you have time and money, such a procedure is both interesting and helpful, but from my accumulated experience I have learned many lessons so simple I can teach you quickly and easily to sketch that idea for the gown you have always wanted.

Get paper, wrapping paper or writing paper, a pencil, scissors, and a fashion plate or magazine. Forget hands, faces, and feet; the main thing we are to put over is the idea of a dress and for this, only the silhouette (the outline of a dress reduced to its simplest lines) is important. I suggest that you cut, paper-doll-like, a figure from a fashion magazine—a figure about 6 inches high with an arm swung away from the body, since it is easier for a beginner to sketch a sleeve on a free arm, and, of course, only one sleeve need be sketched. This same paper-doll silhouette may be used over and over again as your outline. In each figure which follows on page 21, observe the original silhouette. Figures B and C show how designs may be placed on

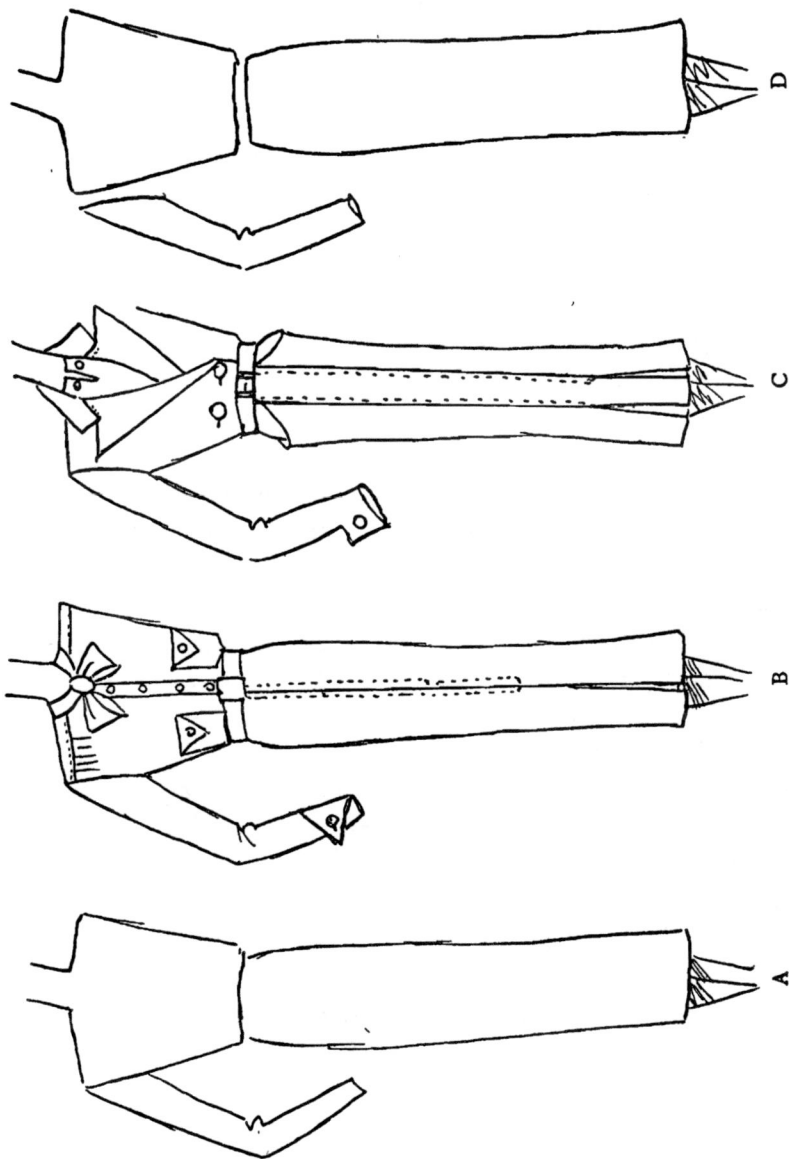

FIGURES USING THE SAME BASIC SILHOUETTE

the basic silhouette. After the dress is sketched the outline figure (the foundation lines) may be erased, if its lines are confusing.

If you want to learn to draw your silhouette free-hand, sketch each part separately as shown in silhouette D. Note that the shoulders are broad and taper down to the waist. The hip is slightly broader than the skirt. The arm or sleeve is simple. Put these together and you have the silhouette A.

But how does one go about the intricate details which make a dress look like a dress? On page 23 you will find a complete assortment of the curliques you need. In all your sketches of collars, bows, pleated skirts, jabots, etc., etc., these are the foundation lines. To perfect your skill, try making them when you haven't anything else to do, just as folks used to practice Spencerian handwriting or stenography. Make each one twenty times before trying the next. This practice is necessary to accustom your hand to the swing of making them. Use your pencil lightly; never use hard lines.

Notice that drawing 1 is like a lot of *u*'s or *m*'s run together; drawing 2 is very much the same except that each *u* is square at the top and bottom; drawing 3 is the same as drawing 1 but the spacing is wider. Drawing 4 is a capital E with an extra tail. The lines of drawing 5 are made from the bottom up. Your pencil should be released quickly to accomplish the tapered line at the top. When these lines are

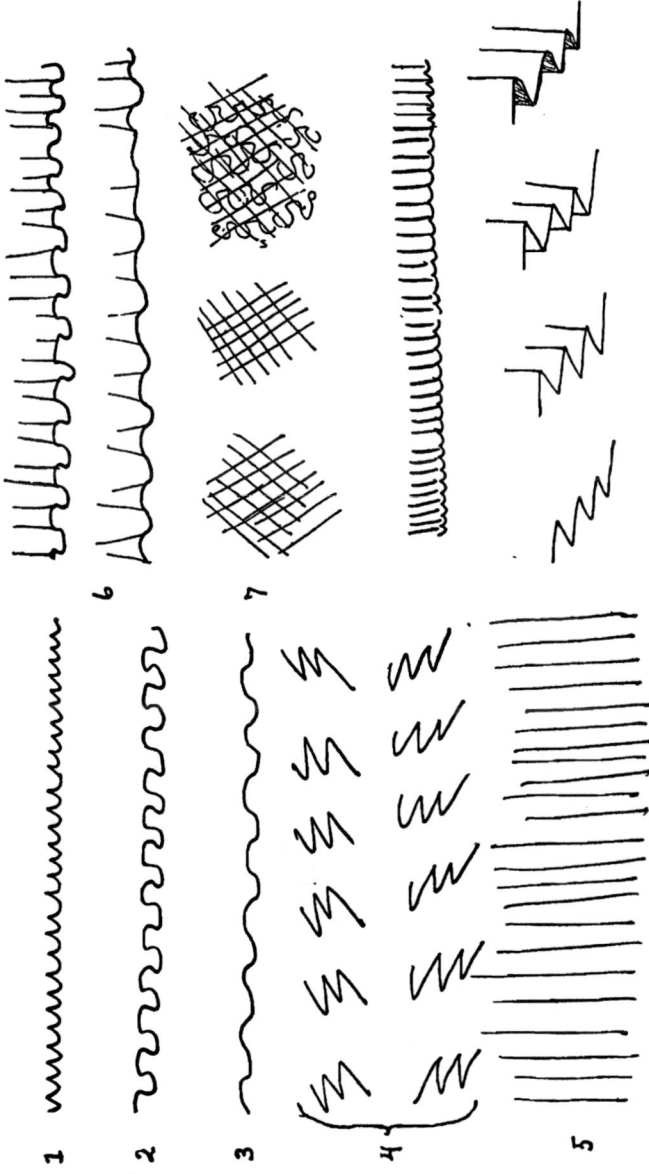

BASIC DRAWINGS USED IN SKETCHING DETAILS OF DRESS

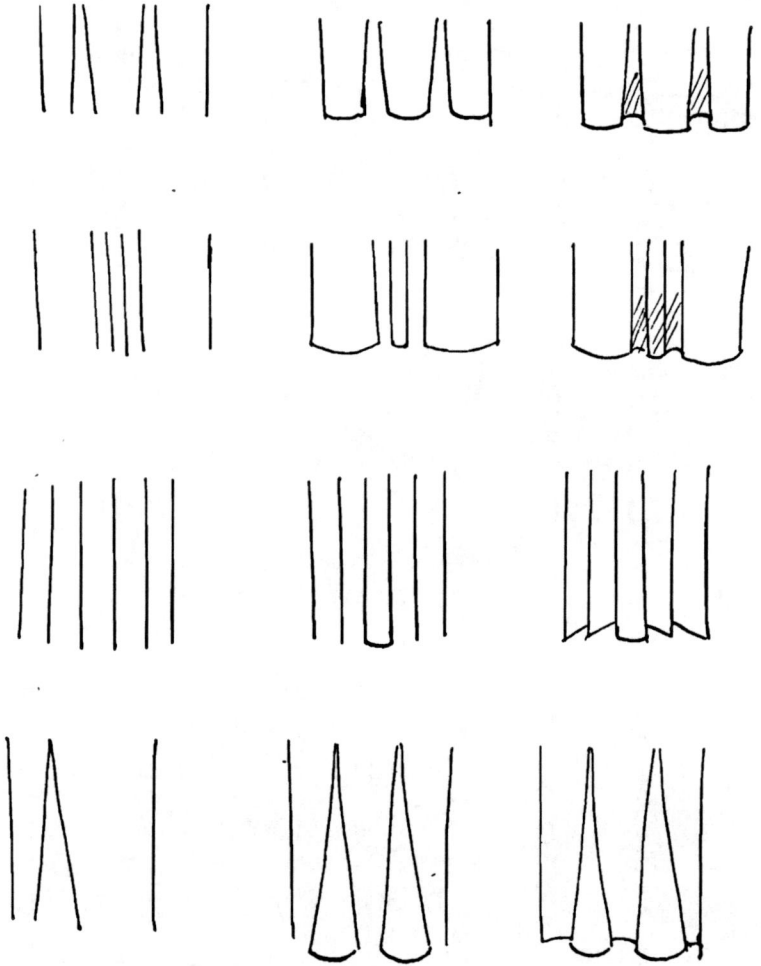

PRACTICE SHEET FOR BOTTOM OF SKIRTS

24

SKETCHING YOUR OWN DRESS

PRACTICE SHEET USING BASIC DRAWINGS

applied to drawings 1, 2, 3, and 4, we have the effects shown in drawing 6, used to illustrate ruffles, box pleats, hems, knife pleats, and flares. Drawing 7 shows the two markings used in illustrating lace. When the crisscross marks of drawing 7 are made over drawing 2, we have a lacy effect. See page 23.

I will refer to these seven drawings many times for they are necessary in the sketching of all dresses. Now in the drawings on the opposite page, identify and analyze the lines used to sketch the separate parts. Try drawing, separately, jabots, the hem of a box-pleated skirt, ruffles, etc., to get the feel of making them before you start the sketch of a whole garment. (You might copy the figures on pages 24, 25, and 27.)

You will next want to know how to sketch accessories, of which collars, bows, cuffs, belts, pockets, buttons, flowers, tucking, ruching, scarf, and lace, are the most common.

While it is true that accessories often make a dress, try, above all things, not to over-trim your dress. It is, to say the least, the extreme in bad taste. I recall a woman in a small Kentucky town who came to a party dressed in a blue evening gown with a pink satin sash, a bunch of wild flowers on her shoulder, two plumes in her hair, bracelets enough for several people, and a string of pearls around her neck. The eyes of one of our Kentucky gentlemen followed her across the room. "Looks

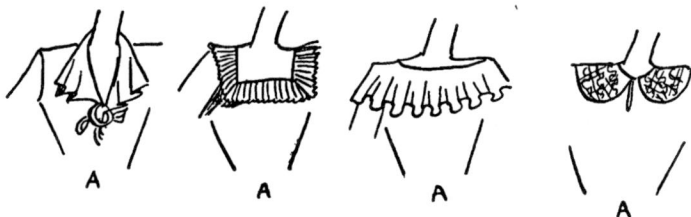

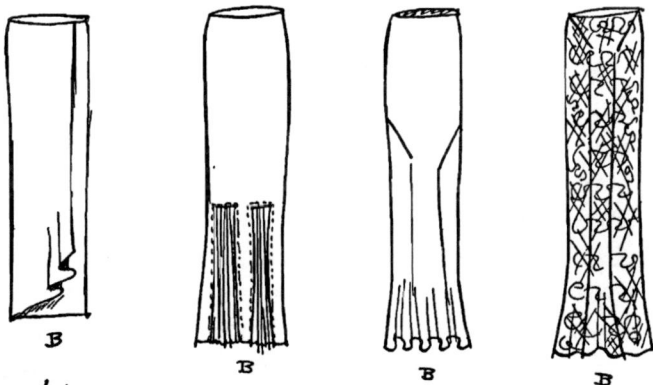

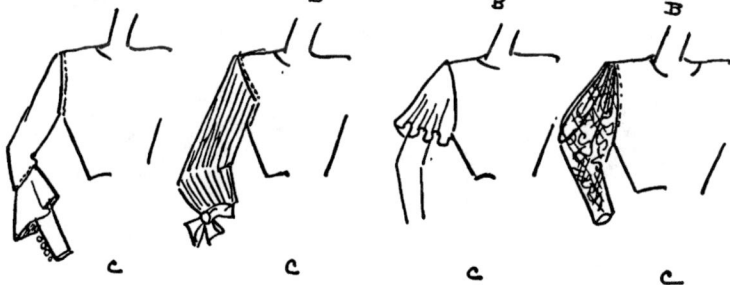

PRACTICE SHEET FOR BASIC DRAWINGS

27

to me," said he with that famous Southern drawl, "like Susie kinda overtended to herself." The gown she wore was lovely in itself; would have been charming without "accessories." So I stress the fact that the more simple your garment, the more striking and the better your appearance. If you use a jabot you do not need flowers, if you use flowers, you do not need a jabot. Don't "overtend" to yourself.

Accessories are drawn by using the seven basic sketches shown on page 23, simple to make if you follow instructions.

Bows. Start your bow with a large O. Now draw a straight line, on either side, dropping slightly down. Add a narrow loop on either side at a parallel slope. Join the ends of line and loop, add two more lines on either side to show the bow-ends falling under. Close these with E lines, as shown in sketch 4 and shade them to give your bow softness.

Flowers. Only a few conventional flowers are used in sketching. The rose is the most common and the easiest to draw. Start at the center with a tiny circle, enlarging in spiral fashion until the rose is the size you wish. Add two or three pointed leaves and a stem.

28

Buttons, Buttonholes, and Buckles. Buttons may be various sizes and shapes—round, oblong, square, etc. In sketching them, first draw your button and then to the left, and on a line with the button center, add a narrow loop illustrating the buttonhole. Dot the button with the number of "eyes" it is to have.

Follow the same general idea in the sketching of buckles.

Lace and Net. Refer to page 23. Notice that when the crisscross marks of drawing 7 are applied over the marks in drawing 2, the effect is that of lace or net.

Ruching. To draw ruching, use drawing 1 or 2 combined with drawing 5.

29

Pockets. Patch pockets may be square, tri-angular, cone-shaped, or round.

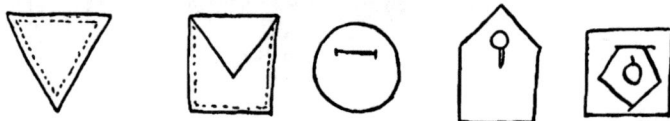

Monograms. Your monogram may be sketched in different styles, futuristic, Chinese, triangulars, etc., or you may sketch a motif resembling a monogram, but having only a conventional design.

Tucking. To illustrate tucking use straight lines paralleled with dotted lines.

SKETCHING YOUR OWN DRESS

Shirring. For drawing shirring, use three rows of drawing 1, combined with the lines of drawing 5.

Jackets. In drawing a jacket, notice that, no matter what length, it swings slightly away from the skirt to give the appearance of being separate. Also note how the lapels are added, using the E

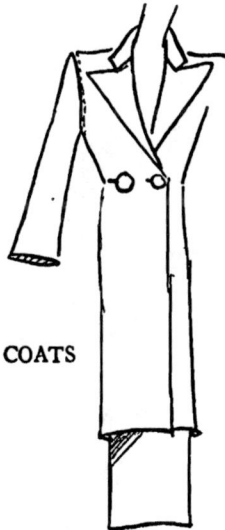

CARDIGAN, BOX, AND THREE-QUARTER COATS

sketch. The sleeve is finished with an oval at the hand. (See page 31.)

Designs shown on pages 25, 29, and 43 can be used for practice in drawing accessories. The sketches below are designs used in sketching the patterns used in dress materials.

DESIGNS USED IN DRESS MATERIALS

SKETCHING YOUR OWN DRESS

Now that you have learned the sketching of both silhouette and accessories, we shall design a dress which you can really carry out. In any one season the number of silhouettes (the actual foundation patterns) used in making the many, many dresses are few. It is good practice to go through a fashion magazine and consider the different foundation patterns. Pick out the one which best suits you. Now shop about among all the illustrations for the ideas you wish to use. You will notice that sleeves, neck, and belt make the dress and that the possibility of variation in these details is endless.

Shall your dress have a V or a square neck? Short or long sleeves? Shall it have a plain shirt or one with kick pleats or flares?

On page 34 are three designs each of which seems entirely different from the others, but which uses the same basic silhouette. In truth they differ only in sleeves, neck, and belt.

Let me here repeat that not all the ideas for your costume have to come out of a fashion book. Perhaps you will wish to go to the neck-wear department of some store to see the latest styles and materials for collars and cuffs, ruffles, frills, vests, etc. Or to the belt department to see if you want a ready-made belt of suede, pique, or patent leather.

After a while the best ideas should come from your own clever brain, but first steep yourself in

ideas! Some day you are sure to find yourself sketching, entirely on your own, the dress of your heart's
desire! Once you have sketched a complete dress,

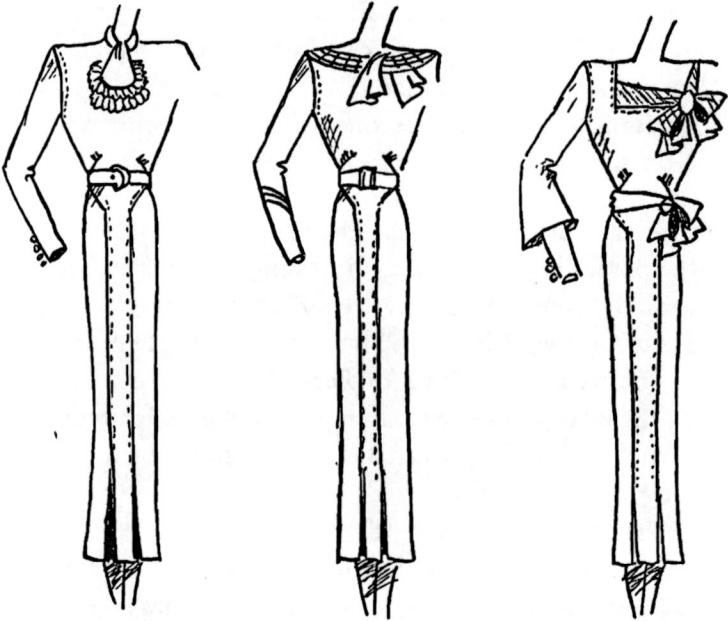

you will find yourself able to carry in your mind
details of your dresses you see in shops, at teas,
at the theatre.

On page 35, are separately sketched four skirts,
four sleeves, and four necklines. Assemble a dress
using one of each· for your practice, choose and
combine your favorites.

34

SKETCHING YOUR OWN DRESS

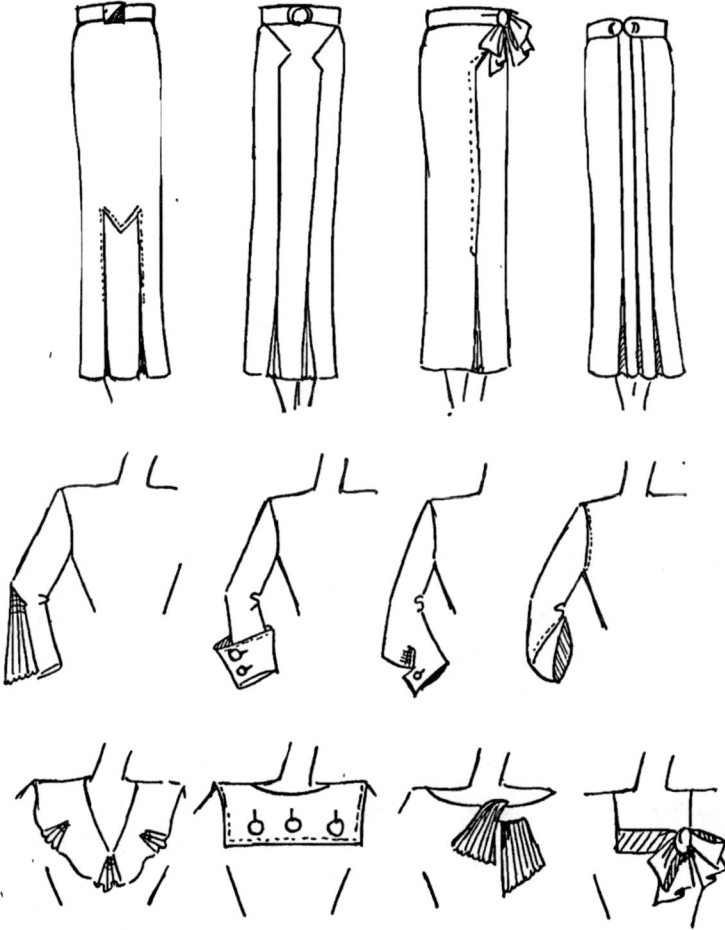

SUGGESTIONS FOR SKETCHING A DRESS

CUTTING AND ASSEMBLING

NOW that your sketch is made, you will want to purchase a foundation pattern to serve as your guide. I cannot possibly instruct you in following all this or any other season's patterns, but I shall consider one pattern very fully from which example you will be able to use any you select.

Buy a two-piece skirt pattern, a pattern of a blouse, and a plain long sleeve. (You may be able to find the three in one pattern.) Cut the five parts out of muslin, an old sheet, or some other old material, preferably white, and baste them together. Slip this garment on and, with someone helping you, fit it perfectly to your figure by basting or with pins.

If you are inexperienced with the needle, it will be easier for you to drape and fit your dress on a form, or dummy, so that you can see yourself as "ithers" see you. If you can't afford a ready-made form you can make one for very little cost.

Buy a few yards (about 3½ for an average size) of heavy canvas, the kind used to cover an ironing-board. This may be purchased in any department store. From this canvas cut a pattern which may be fitted snugly to your body .Cut off at about knee length. Hold it (as if standing on the floor) on a like piece of material while someone assisting you draws around it marking a piece which may be cut and sewed in the opening. Leave the neck open, stuff with excelsior, then close. Mount this on **a**

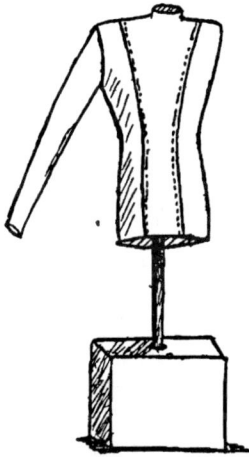

HOMEMADE DUMMY

broomstick which has been run through a well-made box. Weighting the box will help give the dummy a substantial footing. The seams of the dummy are the same back and front. If you want an arm, take your long one-piece sleeve pattern, sew it up, stuff it, and sew it to the shoulder of the dummy.

Now, to continue with the making of your pattern. With the basted five-part garment either on

37

yourself or on the form, the next step is to outline, in pencil or crayon, on the material, the lines you have used in your sketch. Suppose you have designed A and the foundation pattern which you purchased for it looks like B. Then C shows the

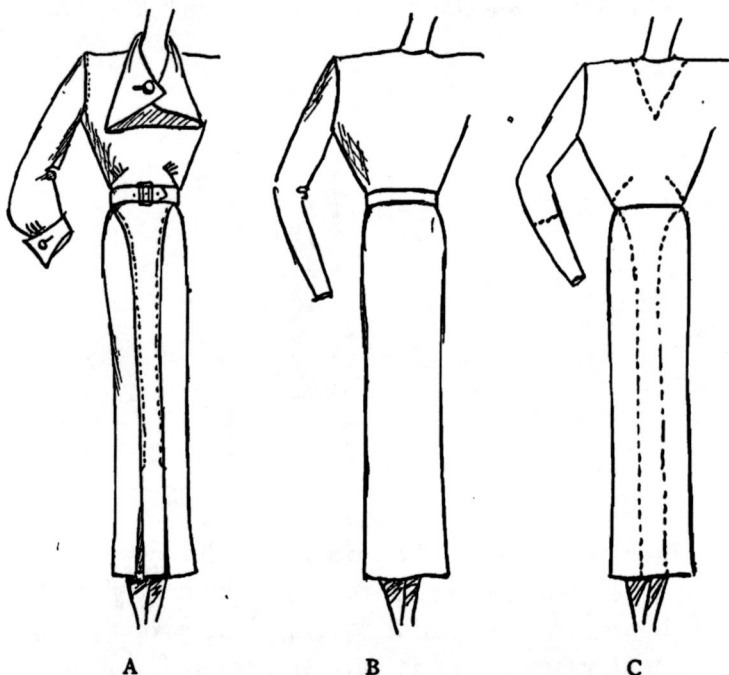

A   B   C

foundation which you have basted together with the lines of your original design, drawn upon it. Compare A and C. C shows the V-neck, the three-quarter sleeve, and the pleats.

Now you are ready to take this garment apart to use as your actual pattern. Open the seams and

38

cut the pattern where you have drawn the dotted lines. Your foundation pattern shows a V-neck which should be cut first, and there is something very important to remember here; your new pattern does not allow seams along the dotted lines, so in cutting the material for your dress *allow for a one-inch seam where there is a dotted line.*

You bought a pattern with a long sleeve but your sketch shows one of three-quarter length with a puff below the elbow. How are you to make such a transformation? You will have to cut a

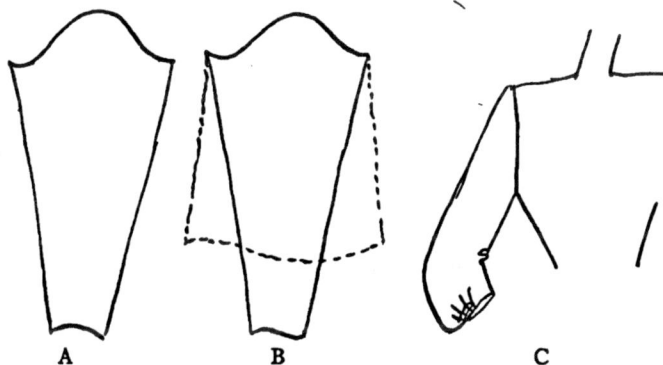

A   B   C

new pattern. Take the sleeve from your foundation pattern or dress, open the seams, and lay it on another piece of muslin or paper as shown in Fig. B. Swing out the pattern to the dotted lines, to give the needed fullness, and cut the muslin off three-quarter length. When this sleeve is sewed together, it will look like Fig. C. Note that the top of the sleeve remains the same.

39

But suppose you want a sleeve with the puff at the top. Cut a slightly oval top of muslin, as shown in Fig. A below. Gather the top of the sleeve, Fig. B. Now place the sleeve of your foundation pattern over the gathered material Fig. C and cut it. This will give you the sleeve shown in Fig. D.

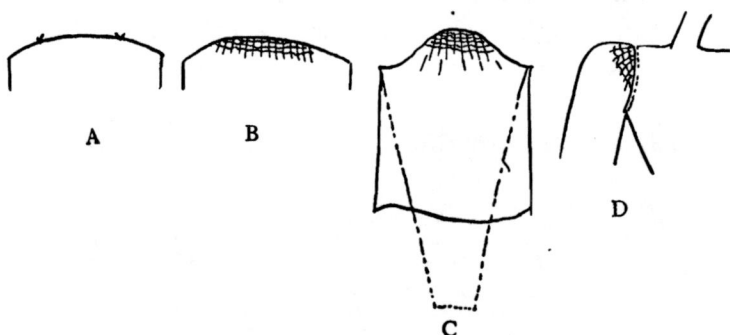

A   B   C   D

Your sketch also shows that you want kick pleats. With your foundation skirt pattern (page 41) laid on your new material, cut the square extension shown at the bottom of the skirt A. This will fold under to form the pleat when the skirt is sewed together again as shown in B.

Remember that you must allow for a one-inch seam.

Now about cutting patterns for your accessories— collars, cuffs, belts, etc. It's true you can find many beautiful accessories in the department stores, both inexpensive and otherwise, but it is fun to make your own and you will enjoy developing your

40

own talent. Take muslin, or even ordinary wrapping paper, and do a little experimenting. Cut the pattern free-hand until you get the shape you want. For example, you have decided on illustrations A (p. 42) for your collar, belt, and cuffs. Study them as they look in the sketch and then try cutting

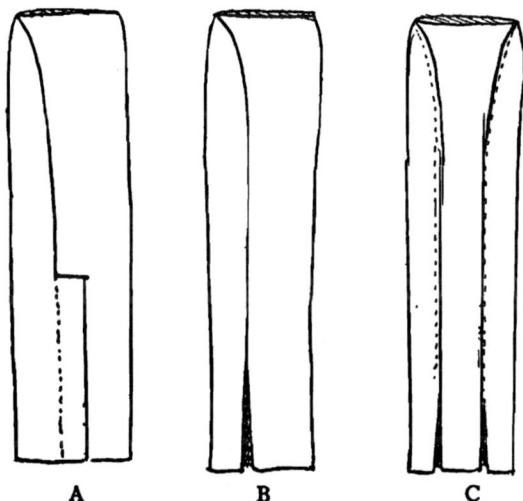

A   B   C

them of paper. Fit the paper pattern around your neck and arm, or on your dummy, until you have the measurements exactly the right size. If it is too large, pin little pleats in it. Work with this paper pattern until the inside measurement of the collar is the same size as the neck of the dress. Then you can be sure the collar will not be too large or ripple. Illustrations B show how the collar and cuff of your sketch will look in pattern form.

41

There is no set rule for making accessories. At first it may be a little difficult to cut them, but, like working a cross-word puzzle, after a while

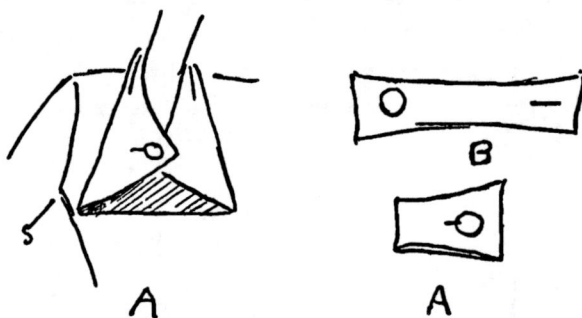

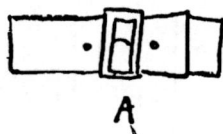

it becomes a hobby. On pag 43 are a number of collars of different styles. Practice cutting and fitting them just to get the knack. Take a square about the size of a man's handkerchief, cut a hole

42

CUTTING AND ASSEMBLING

VARIETY IN NECKLINES

43

in the center, and see what type of collar you can make. Cut the corners off and you have another style. Keep experimenting with the scissors to see how many different styles you can make.

Now every detail of your dress is in pattern form. The moment has come for cutting the material. This should be a real pleasure and should not frighten you so badly that you cannot cut carefully, for cutting, too, is an art and must be done skillfully and accurately. By now you should see that each step is rather simple and that if you follow directions you are not going to fail. My first attempts in making clothes at home were most disconcerting, discouraging, and difficult. What nerve-racking hours I would have saved myself, had I only known then what I know now about the simplified methods I have learned (and often have invented) in the wholesale trade where simplicity not complicity is the professional keynote.

FIT OR MISFIT

IF WE judge by what we see every day a great
many women do not know their own figures;
—have no idea of their size. Considering the
great variety of dresses on the market at reasonable
prices, made in standard sizes, over-sizes, and half-
sizes, and the extreme care with which patterns are
made, there is really no need for any woman to look
as though she had been squeezed into her clothes
nor, on the other hand, as though she were wearing a
mother hubbard, or a bungalow apron. Yet this is
what we see every day and shall continue to see until
women are honest with themselves and apply common sense to the selection of their clothes, and when
I say honest that is really what I mean. The older
woman who insists on getting herself rigged out in
a junior-miss costume regardless of her size is still
living her adolescence. The fat woman who bulges
at every seam won't believe she is fat. All of us
have seen the scrawny woman who, regardless of
type, wears a "girl scout" style of dress, no more
suited to her than a sailor suit is to the Peter Arno
type.

Clothes are designed to keep every woman as
youthful looking as possible, but there is no point

in going to extremes. Styles for the young girl and
the matron differ little but this little is all-important,
for it takes into account just what we are considering—the difference in figures. I have heard women
say complainingly: "The styles this year are not
becoming to me. They are all intended for the very
young girl, or the slender woman," etc. Women who
make these remarks have not been sufficiently
observant. They haven't given the matter thought
or they would realize that designers, pattern-
makers, or dress manufacturers could not afford to
disregard any type of figure. You probably know,
that there are special houses which cater only to
one type of figure: the over-size, or the half-size,
or regular sizes, etc., and every year new styles
are adapted to these figures. If you feel despondent
about the season's styles hunt further for your type.
You have not been forgotten.

Another reason why we see grotesquely attired
people on the streets is that some women gain or
lose weight rapidly and their figures actually change,
but they go blissfully along unconsciously bulging
out or shrinking up, as the case may be, wearing the
same type of clothes.

Few women realize what an important part in
the adding to or subtracting from their size is played
by the kind of fabric worn. Nappy, rough wools, or
heavy crepes make the slender person seem considerably heavier, while plain, smooth weaves in

both wool and silk help the stout figure to appear slender. Fluffy materials, organdie, taffeta, and the like, are becoming to the thin type; voils, flat crepes, and smooth weaves in wool are better for the larger figure. Choice of fabric, then, should be given careful consideration. Let the material relieve the lines of your garment from carrying the entire burden of making you look slender or more rounded, whichever effect you are trying to attain.

One of the very good reasons why you should learn to cut your own clothes is that you can take into account the adjustment needed. Practically every figure calls for at least a slight alteration in the pattern. We really should be glad there is still a little chance for individuality in a world of standardization. If you are making a dress or buying one, it will be helpful to know your measurements and where you deviate from the average. This will also aid you in deciding whether a dress can be altered satisfactorily. Pattern-makers are beginning to realize women's need for a greater variety of sizes and are putting out half-sizes and standard sizes with varying hip and bust measurements. As you know, the standard sizes begin with 12, 14, 16, and run to 40, 42, 44, etc., and junior-miss sizes with 11, 13, 15 and on to 17, but these do not fit perfectly every figure for which they are intended. Your waist may be a trifle shorter, your sleeve a little longer than the average.

47

HOW TO DESIGN YOUR OWN CLOTHES

If you are really interested in appearing well dressed, you will know all these facts about your figure and will have your clothes fitted accordingly. Remember that, no matter what your size, you will look well dressed, if your dress fits the figure you possess, and not the one you wish you had. Too often if your clothes are not satisfactory, the fault lies not with the color, material, or style, but with fitting.

What I am about to say in regard to the principle of dress, always has been true and always will be true, and is a factor which is taken into account by every builder of styles—Parisian or American. It is based on a universal law—the law of opposites—and applies not only to clothes design but to architecture, painting, and the like. The artist wishing to lessen the gloom of his picture creates a lighter tone. The architect designing a high tower gives balance to the structure by using lower transepts and buttresses. Each achieves in his own way the balance his work demands by supplying the opposite quality.

Let this principle apply to the idea of dress. If you are inclined to be too broad, work to use lengthwise (perpendicular) lines in your sketch. If you are tall, break your height with crosswise (horizontal) lines. Do not use too many conflicting lines or you will defeat your purpose. To illustrate how this is actually done, let us take the four outstanding types and a shading: the short-stout, the tall-stout,

48

the short-slender, the tall-slender, and the junior-miss.

SAME DRESS USING HORIZONTAL AND PERPENDIDULAR LINES

The Short-Stout. The short stout person's problem is to achieve height. Her costume must

49

feature perpendicular lines, avoiding lines which go crosswise. The heart-shaped, low-round, and V-neck which do emphasize the right lines obviously are best. The V-neck especially makes the face look thinner and softens its lines. High, square, or round lines reduce the stout person's height and exaggerate the roundness of her face. The three-quarter sleeve gives length, and the long, straight one still more length. However, the latter must not be too tight. Many women evidently do not know what is meant by "too tight." Perhaps I can illustrate by telling you a story my aunt once told me about a beau she had when a girl; in the days when, to be in the height of fashion, a young man's breeches were nothing if not snug. The first evening that "certain" young man called in his new clothes, even his most cautious bending into the best parlor hair-cloth resulted in split trousers—and the next day a severe upbraiding for the tailor. Said the tailor, "But you told me to make them skin tight." "I know," said the young man, "but I can sit down in my skin." Comfort in clothes demands that they do not fit so tightly we cannot bend our elbows or tie our own shoelaces.

A loose bell or slightly flared sleeve is becoming to the short stout woman and is comfortable, especially in warm weather. Short puffed sleeves give a boxed appearance and should be avoided by all stout persons. A full-length coat gives height to the short woman, while box coats and three-quarter ones make her look stocky. Short coats should be fitted. Strange as this may seem, the bolero jacket makes the figure of the short-stout seem taller and more slender. There is reason for this—it gives greater length to the skirt by allowing all the perpendicular lines to be exposed. Peplums add to her width and are unbecoming. Pleats and flares in skirts, if inserted at the waist line and extended to the bottom of the hem, will add height; if they are inserted at the knee or below, they shorten the figure considerably.

But the short-stout may follow the correct styles, achieve all the correct lines, and still have an unattractive costume if she has chosen the wrong kind of material. Subdued, one-tone, or small-figured material should be worn by the short stout woman if she is to look well dressed. Horizontal stripes were never intended for her and she should avoid heavy weaves with rough finishes.

The Tall-Stout. The tall stout woman is often considered handsome. In spite of her weight she can be very attractive if she chooses her clothes with care. Low necklines, either surplice or draped in cowl fashion, or V effects are especially flattering. Fussy, frilled clothes with ornate accessories give her an awkward, over-dressed appearance. Sleeves soft and flowing from the elbow or below, but never puffed at the armhole, are becoming to her. The

51

long straight sleeve is excellent if not too snugly fitted. The single-breasted coat is more flattering than the double-breasted one. The wrap-around skirt and the coat dress with their straight lines can also be worn. The tall stout person can wear short, three-quarter, or long coats, all of which should be at least slightly fitted. Skirts with long straight lines are the most graceful. Straight pleats and flares which begin at the normal waist-line and continue to the bottom of the skirt, allowing the fullness to be released at about the knee, are very becoming. For evening wear, short narrow trains are flattering. The large waist-line should be kept as inconspicuous as possible. The belt should never be noticeable; the same fabric of which the dress is made is best. Lingerie cuffs and collars may be worn if they lie flat. Vestees can be worn well.

It is the concern of the stout woman to avoid wearing a garment which fits too closely, but to see that it is made snug enough not to appear baggy.

The Short-Slender. Being slender and being thin are two different things. If you are thin try and disguise the fact. Nothing is more unattractive than the thin girl or woman with a dress cut too low, especially in the back; a capital reminder of a washboard. However, if you are *slender* and give thought to planning your clothes, you have an advantage over girls and women with other types of figures, for there are so many styles designed for you.

The short-slender woman or girl can afford to be more daring in regard to necklines and sleeve treatments. However, it is wise to bear in mind that simple lines belong to all types. The slender figure can afford to wear box-coats and puffed sleeves—puffed either at the elbow or at the hand. Double-breasted jackets and coats are worn well for they add width and keep the figure from looking too slim. This figure can wear coats of varying lengths, fitted or loose. Kick pleats inserted at or below the knee are becoming, as is also the plain straight skirt. Sailor collars or high collars, ruffles at the neck, large cuffs or gauntlet effect can be worn effectively. The close-fitting buster brown collar or any other kind of collar buttoned up to the throat is becoming. The short-slender figure can wear a great variety of fabrics: tweeds or closely-woven materials; large-flowered, striped, or plain patterns. This type must remember to use lines that do not accentuate her shortness.

The Tall-Slender. The tall-slender girl is usually the envy of the other types. Her problems are much less difficult than those of the types already discussed.

The V, square, or boat (sometimes called the Jenny) neckline is flattering to the tall-slender person. High or low necklines, with cowls or with bows, and the soft draped necklines are particularly hers. Frills about the neck and sleeves

53

are well suited to this type. If the arm is not too slender, any length sleeve may be worn. Sleeves puffed at the armhole give a broad shoulder line and cut the appearance of height. She may also wear a long flowing or draped sleeve. Sleeves cut raglan style or with deep armholes give effective lines to her costume. The tall slender figure can wear a variety of skirts—skirts with box-pleats inserted at the knee, with inverted pleats running from waistline to hem; or with flounces and flares. The tall figure is really the only type to carry with style a bias skirt. Tunics and peplums are very becoming to the tall slender woman. Her coats may be three-quarter length, hip-length (finger-tip), or long. If long, they should be slightly fitted. Box or swagger coats may be worn. The tall thin girl should wear fabrics which help to "fill her out." Tweeds and coarse weaves are suitable.

The Junior-Miss. The variety of colors, materials, and styles appropriate to the junior-miss make her clothes fascinating. This young lady can wear extreme and exaggerated styles or the plainer sportswear. Her wardrobe can run the gamut of style in sleeves, necklines, skirts, and accessories. She can certainly wear a greater variety of colors and materials than the other sizes. Taffetas, chiffons, organdies, crepes; tweed suits, swagger or box coats, double or single-breasted; high and low necklines; frills and furbelows—all belong to her.

54

FIT OR MISFIT

Simple backless and sleeveless frocks are particularly smart on the junior-miss.

With so much attention devoted to her interests
Miss Junior should always look well dressed. Sad
to say, however, this is not the case. Her problem
is not what to wear but when and how to wear it.
The desire for freedom of thought at her age breaks
out savagely in her choice of clothes. Usually the
type of dress the fourteen- or sixteen-year-old
wants to wear is exactly what she should not wear.
My own daughter at the age of fourteen wanted a
black, beaded evening gown which would have been
a charming style for her grandmother. She begged
on another occasion for a "smooth, snaky dress"
with a long train and flowing sleeves.

If you are trying to help the young lady cultivate
clothes-sense, I would suggest that she be allowed
perhaps one of the longed-for inappropriate and
exaggerated creations. Let her look foolish and
ridiculous once or twice. It may be the best way
to teach her to select suitable clothes for herself.
Let her have the black dress. Her "boy-friend"
will tell her more convincingly than could her
mother that she is wearing the wrong style and
color. The real way, however, as I have said before,
to help the young lady learn what to wear and
how to wear it, is to encourage her learning to
design and to make her own clothes.

COLOR AND COLOR COMBINATION

ALMOST every color and variation of color has at some time or other been in vogue in women's clothes. For many years the predominant colors for each season were few and the custom was to rotate the different colors. If maroon, tan, or jade was used one fall, it was pretty certain to be out of vogue the next. Not so nowadays. The variety of colors being used seems inexhaustible compared with the limited selection of even a few years ago, and the use of combinations of color has never been so extensive.

Just as with a popular style, so it is with a popular color. If it is well liked one season, it is a safe prediction that it will be used again, or in such a slightly modified shade that the dress you have will not be entirely out of vogue. Every fall, clothes are featured in brown, green, red, and black; every spring in navy, black, brown, and sometimes red. Grey and tan are used for spring coats. Among the various shades of green, there came a season when lime was exceedingly popular. The next season it was shaded into lettuce and peppermint, and within a few seasons lime, lettuce, leaf, jungle, Patou, jade, Kelly, hunter's green have all been used. This process of change goes on continuously with all colors. The popular yellow shades have been: lemon, peach yellow, mustard, gold, corn, maize; red shades have ranged through magenta, Oporto, burgundy, beet root, cherry, wine, maroon, watermelon, cerise. Combinations of these shades make an endless variety.

It is interesting and amusing how colors are given such unusual names and how fads come into fashion. Do you recall how a few years ago the finding of the Tutank-ah-men tomb influenced fabric and design? In June of this year when the United States fleet was in New York for a visit, sailor blue was featured in every shop window on Fifth Avenue and youngsters—boys and girls, big and little—donned a sailor cap.

Reminiscent of the Tutank-ah-men fad is a story which at that time went the rounds of the dress trade. A manufacturer who made a noticeable success using this particular pattern inspired one of his competitors to try it also. Several hundred yards of material with the Tut design were rushed through into dresses, but alas the heyday of the fad had passed and with it, the orders. Week in and out the dresses stayed on the racks. One evening, the stock boy said to his boss, "Shall I cover up the Tuts tonight?" "Nar," growled the disgusted dealer, "don't cover 'em, separate 'em! They multiply over night." ·

57

HOW TO DESIGN YOUR OWN CLOTHES

The chief explanation of so many shades being worn at present is that women have overcome their timidity in using color. The housewife no longer works in a drab kitchen but in one that glows with color (for, after all, colors are just as immaculate as white and much more cheerful). When her work is done, she may quite probably be driving forth in a car of vivid blue, or tan with green wheels, or grey trimmed with crimson. Color has invaded so many parts of her life that she has learned to use it effectively and extensively.

Women have also learned how clothes and colors can affect moods—how changing to a more colorful, or a more becoming, dress can summon a veritable holiday spirit, a miracle not to be treated lightly. We can actually have more real enjoyment of our food, if we change from work dress to dinner dress, and when we are not feeling our best let us at least wear the color that makes us look our best.

You can recall the staid notions of the older generation in regard to color in clothes: red, light blue, or light pink were only for the young woman; lavender, grey, or black only for the woman mature and grey-haired. A red-haired girl or woman should never wear red; a fair-haired girl should never wear brown. Ideas, however, entirely *passé*. Last season, the junior-miss wore black evening dresses and linen or black taffeta jackets; the grey-haired women wore watermelon red or any vivid shade she chose. The young woman with grey hair is so enchanting in vivid shades that she has given the older woman courage to wear them also.

But many of us find ourselves in a middle or in-between group, neither distinctly blonde, brunette, red-haired, or grey-haired, nor do we possess the complexion which usually accompanies a given type. A woman may have titian hair but not the florid complexion that generally goes with it, or she may have coal-black hair and blue eyes. These variations undoubtedly make the color problem more difficult for there can be no set rules about what will be most becoming. As many shades, however, may be worn by the in-between types as by the usual types, and often tones with more distinctive effect.

Among the in-between types, have you ever noticed the girl whose eyes are a greyish-greenish blue? It is hard to tell which color predominates. To watch her eyes take on the color of her dress is fascinating: if she wears green, her eyes become green, if she wears blue, they are blue, but brown produces just eyes—nondescript and colorless. Not all of us can change our eyes so completely but we can emphasize the color of both eyes and our complexion more than most of us do.

To discuss all the variations in types of beauty and what colors are best suited to each would be endless, but perhaps I may at least suggest how

59

to select flattering colors. First of all, experiment. It was experimenting which proved that the golden-haired girl can wear red, that the flaxen-haired girl is stunning in black. A good plan is to try a new color in a jacket, scarf, hat, or blouse, or some other fairly inexpensive garment. Give yourself a chance to feel comfortable in it. Ask the opinion of your friends, and don't overlook the fact that though men may be conservative in opinions on style, they nevertheless seem instinctively to know and, best of all, will tell you if a style or color is becoming.

Experiment with the color in question near your face to discover what it does to your eyes, your hair, and your skin. Red is not becoming to a red-haired woman because it gives her a faded appearance. The colors you wear should bring out your best qualities. Try new combinations. Usually the color which flatters you most is the one you like best.

Remember that combination of the right colors is an art and needs careful study. While many combinations are in vogue, there is a limit to the number of colors which may be successfully combined. Two, and less often three, colors may be used together in a dress; for scarfs and other accessories more than two may be combined harmoniously. Of the recent popular tones you will find that lime green and royal blue make an arresting combination, as do soft yellow and royal blue. Peach pink is beautiful used with deep chocolate brown as is also blue of the aquamarine shade; sailor or royal blue with black and white, deep wine with dusty pink. There was a time when brown was used only with tan. We are now wearing brown with blue, with grey, and, best of all, with white. Modern art has shown us that color and color combinations have untold possibilities.

I hesitate to classify colors according to their becomingness to different types of beauty: blondes, brunettes, red heads, and grey heads. These classifications seem to take into account the hair particularly, though, the color of skin and eyes carry equal weight in arriving at a decision. My opinion, while based on years of experience in dealing with women of all the types, is only my opinion and should not be considered unchangeable, for, of course, there are exceptions to every rule.

Blondes I have found usually look attractive in all tones of blue. Black, navy, and brown are also becoming. Nearly all pastel shades and red can be worn if the blonde is fair skinned.

Brunettes with fair skin look lovely in shades of purple, periwinkle blue (a soft purplish blue), black, red, green, and all vivid shades. The dark-skinned brunette should be careful in wearing subdued shades and should avoid purple and deeper shades of red.

The *red-head* has much more freedom in the use of color than formerly. She is usually striking and

61

most attractive if she has chosen her colors wisely. Greens, rust tones, brown, and almost any pastel shade, with the exception of pink, belong to her.

Grey hair is now in fashion. The young lady with "silver threads among the gold," or among the brown or black no longer dyes her hair. The natural color, whatever shade or mixture, gives her face softer lines and aids her considerably in choosing the right tones. Grey, brown, and tan are not becomingly worn with grey hair unless they are relieved with a dash of vivid color. Blue, purple, wine, green, and all pastel shades are lovely on gray-haired women—young, middle-aged, or elderly.

I hope some of you may have the fun I experienced in discovering for myself a new and becoming color. One day when shopping on the Avenue I came across a purple suit with grey caracul collar— so "different," so beautiful! But I had never worn any shade of purple in my life. To me purple was an old lady's color; tucked away in my memory was a picture of grandmother in a purple dress with a lace collar. But the suit with caracul was too delightful not to be tried on. By which accident I discovered the becomingness of purple, bought the suit, of course, and every time I wore it, enjoyed anew the comments of my friends. "Have you lost weight?" they asked. "Have you been away for a rest?" It gave a softness and smoothness to my complexion, light to my dark brown hair that no other shade has even given and since this experience, each season I have an outfit of some tone of purple, whether or not it is among the season's favorites.

From my own experience, my advice would certainly be: if you find a becoming color wear it regardless of fad or fashion.

ECONOMY MEASURES

(REMAKES AND DOUBLE-DUTY CLOTHES)

SINCE the depression has come upon us, we have seen the old adage of the ill wind dramatized in many different settings. All have by no means been tragic. Depression days have "brought out" many persons, especially women whose lives I am certain would still be drab and uninteresting had not necessity driven them to become ingenious and creative. They have found beauty in the commonplace. They have learned to do things which make them interesting to other people, and they are happier for the change.

This "getting down to earth" is reflected in various feminine interests, particularly in the clothes women wear. The extravagance and superficiality expressed in our style standards of a few years ago have disappeared. Today every garment a woman wears does not have to be of expensive material. Still clothes are more attractive and varied than ever before. Women are taking more personal interest in assembling their outfits and the business of dressmaker, which was almost extinct, has been brought to the fore to prosper again.

ECONOMY MEASURES

To most of us economy in clothes means "Do not buy new dresses or hats, but make over old ones." This is one economy measure but there are many more related to clothes. Do you know that there is great economy in planning your entire wardrobe at one time (I did not say buying); in seeing that each dress is planned to serve its purpose to the fullest; in buying material of good quality; and in making or purchasing appropriate and inexpensive accessories?

Only a few days ago I chanced to be lunching downtown and in the rush of the noonday hour was seated with five young matrons, evidently neighbors in a suburban town. The only topic of their conversation was clothes: what kind of materials they were using, how they were making over clothes, what new colors were intriguing, and so on. Since I was forced to be an eavesdropper and wasn't privileged to add my word of wisdom, I listened with amused curiosity, genuinely surprised that women could talk of nothing but clothes for forty minutes, without even so much as mentioning bridge, men, or babies! I have always known that what women wear is one of their chief concerns but this incident brought to me very clearly the angles from which women are thinking and talking of clothes today.

The type of clothes the well-dressed woman should own is determined by her interests and since these are as varied as the colors in vogue, it would be impossible to discuss satisfactorily what belongs in even a few of milady's wardrobes. The need of an approaching season can only be planned for tentatively but the general scheme of coming months at least suggests what we shall want—business clothes, clothes for a Christmas trip, football game, cocktail parties, ad infinitum.

Because it is good sense to begin with what we have I shall first discuss the remaking of things in our stock of old clothes, then take up the making of clothes which give us double and triple service.

When taking inventory of what you have, begin by actually checking with pencil and pad at your wardrobe door. After the inventory is made, plan first for the alteration of old clothes, then for new ones. Suppose, for example, you, the college girl, unearth your last season's tweed suit of brown mixture. Taking this as your starting point, what can you add to your wardrobe to continue using the suit? Here are a few suggestions:

Tweed suit of brown mixture
{
twin sweaters of brown or blue
over-blouse of jersey, linen, or corduroy to match, or contrasting color
lumber-jack shirt
jacket or vest
}

Suppose you are a business girl and have left some very good looking accessories in brown, what might you add next season?

66

Brown shoes { brown and white print dress
" hat { brown and white linen dress
" bag { flowered chiffon dinner dress
" gloves { one-tone brown, green, dusty rose,
aquamarine blue, or maise dress
with plain or print jacket.

Or if your accessories happened to be blue, you might have:

Navy blue hat { navy and white print
" " shoes { white or navy double-duty dress
" " bag { flowered chiffon
" " gloves { pique or gingham street dress

You will see that a wardrobe well planned calls for real study, but the added style which such real study nets you makes it more than worth while.

A dress may be remade to give it complete freshness and variety. The preliminary step is dry-cleaning or washing. This not only lends encouragement to what otherwise might seem a drab task, but also makes the matching of colors and materials easier. A good plan is to study a recent fashion magazine and discover the clear-cut differences between past and present styles. You may find, for example, that skirts are less flared, necklines a bit higher, sleeves tighter. Before ripping the dress apart have your alterations definitely in mind, then sketch your dress with as much care as though it were in its first making. This will help you to discover whether or not the changes you wish to make are possible.

Let's consider some of the more simple altera-

67

tions, applicable to most dresses, taking each part of the foundation pattern, neck, sleeves, and body (waist and skirt) separately.

Necks and Tops. One of the most difficult changes is to build up a neck which was originally low. This can be done by using various styles of vestees or by superimposing a new collar. To raise the neckline wide striped ribbon, stitched to the dress at the back of the neck, may be brought to the front and tied into a bow or looped to form an ascot tie, filling the open front. A high draped cowl neck of contrasting color or fabric added to the dress is also a satisfactory means of accomplishing a raised neckline. It should open at the back of the neck to allow room for the head when putting on the dress.

When the reverse side of materials (dull, satin, or crepey finishes) and contrasting fabrics and colors are in vogue, as they now are, the upper part of the dress can be cut entirely away, and new material used effectively for a reconstructed top. See sketches of double duty dresses, pages 72 and 73. If the original dress is in silk, the new top may be satin, taffeta, or velvet; if the dress is wool, combine it now with knitted fabric or a novelty material.

Sleeves. If the sleeves are worn at the elbow or under the arm this can be taken care of by subtracting the entire sleeve and cutting the neck low. A guimpe of lace, net or other suitable material can be used in their place. Sleeves may be flared by inserting godets or pleats.

68

Altering the length of the sleeves, making short sleeves long, or vice versa, can give a dress an entirely different appearance. Puffs, of course, are more easily taken out than added, but in many cases the sleeve may be reversed, so that a top puff will instead be at the hand—or the fullness which has been at the hand will be at the armhole. Wings, capes, or other shoulder ornaments may be quite simply added or removed to change the style of the dress.

In keeping with style of collar or top, cuffs, of course, must be accordingly changed.

Skirts. If you want to make your skirt longer let the hem down and hand-roll the bottom. If the dress is tailored a one-inch hem may be retained by stitching seam-binding to the edge of the hem and then slip-stitching it to the skirt. Use net or lace to lengthen uneven skirt lengths of soft, flimsy fabrics, particularly the kind used for dinner or evening wear. Skirts may be simply altered at the waist-line by using a peplum or giving the dress a two-piece effect.

If flares are needed in the skirt godets may be inserted. Kick pleats may be added but they should be inserted skillfully to avoid giving the skirt a patched appearance. To make the skirt narrower, rip the seams, and take out the extra fullness. Removable trains have been devised to use for evening wear.

Most of these alterations have in some way

69

called for cutting into the dress, but changes can often be made by changing only the accessories. Collars and cuffs with covered buttons to match may recreate the dress. Changing bone buttons to metal or jeweled ones, adding new clips, using a straight belt in place of a sash, wearing a gay scarf instead of a collar, changing from dark collars and cuffs to crisp white ones—may carry for another season a dress of which you are tired or which you have considered out of style. Many of the accessories found in the department stores may be made economically at home. Shop for ideas as carefully with the re-making of a dress as you did when the dress was "brand" new. Learning to make new accessories for made-over dresses is good practice.

Short jackets or capes added to a costume, give it a dressy appearance. A recent gay style gives us sets of hat, jacket, vest or overblouse, purse, and gloves (or glove tops) made in matching material. For summer they are made of an inexpensive material such as pique, linen, or checked gingham; for fall and winter they are silk, velveteen, or corduroy. For summer these can be worn with the white or pastel colored skirt you probably already have in your wardrobe; for winter they combine nicely with the skirt of tweed, light wool, or velveteen.

There are three types of double-duty dresses: daytime, sports and evening. The evening costume is sleeveless or short sleeved, low-neck or backless, ankle length, with a soft jacket or cape. The more practical type of double-duty dress for daytime usually has a slightly tailored jacket, making the dress suitable for street wear. College girls and women interested in athletics have found the sports' type of double-duty clothes decidedly useful. The student can go to class prepared for a tennis game and the housewife can go marketing, thence to the golf course. Knee-length shorts or pants are attached to a shirt-waist type of blouse and are worn with a wrap-around skirt or one that buttons the full length front or side. These dresses are made of seersucker, pique, gingham, or shirt-maker's goods, and are worn with or without ties, and simple belts of self-material or leather.

Many types of materials and combinations of material lend themselves to double-duty clothes. Some of the combinations of materials which come to mind are: satin and crepe, satin and wool, crepe and print, velvet and metal, taffeta and crepe, taffeta and wool. Light-weight wool jackets and sweaters, with wool dresses, linen jackets with voile dresses, silk dresses with linen jackets, silk jackets and gingham dresses, plain jacket with print dress or vice versa, all make useful combinations.

The style of the jacket has many possibilities. It may be tied at the back of the neck and at the belt, or may button all the way down the back. A jacket with a surplice front which ties at the side is best on a large figure. The close-fitting jacket

71

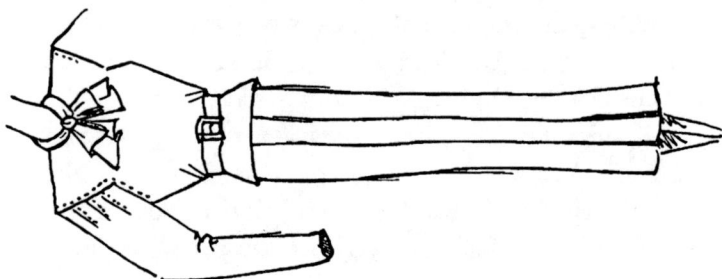

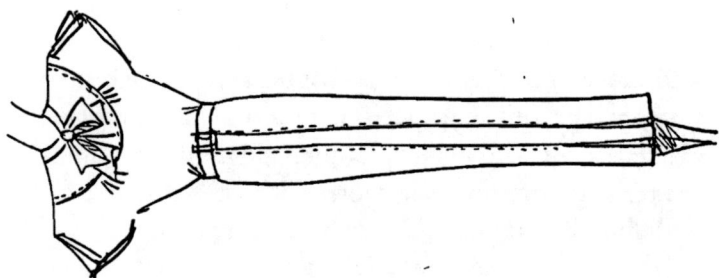

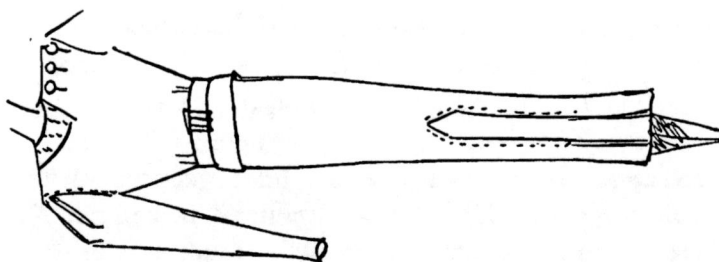

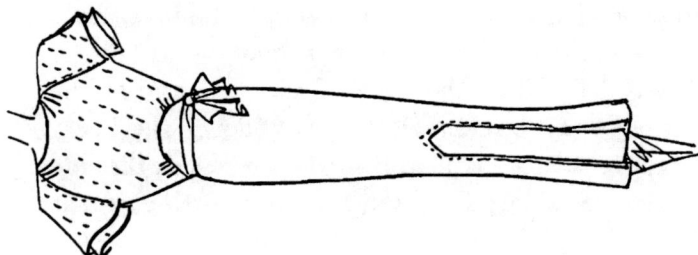

DOUBLE DUTY DRESSES

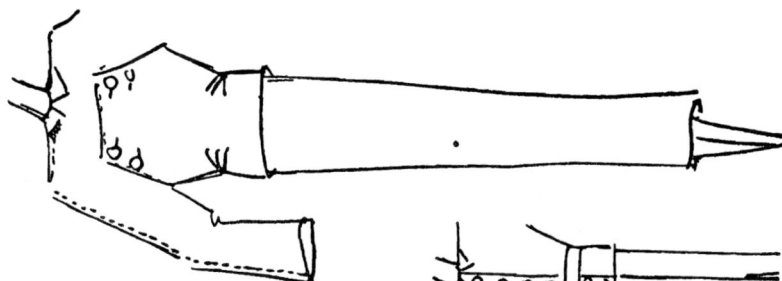

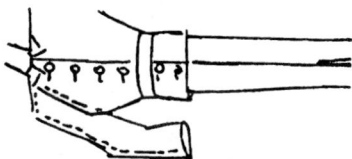

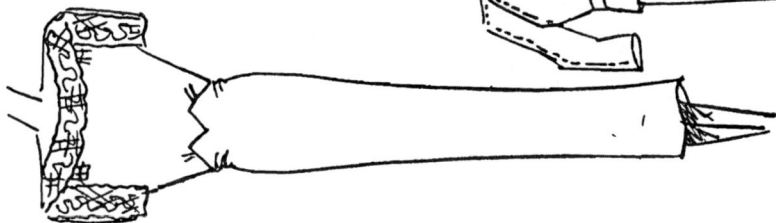

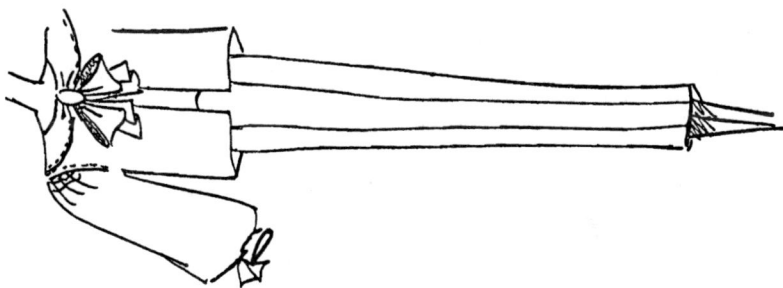

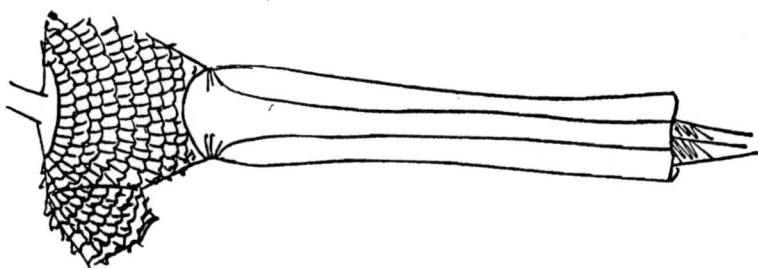

DOUBLE DUTY DRESSES

73

buttoning at the throat is becoming to the slender type. In order to see double-duty dresses with and without jackets consider the four styles on page 72 and 73.

Earlier, I have said that buying material of good quality is economical. The reason for this is that good material can generally stand the wear and tear of active use. It does not stretch or pull at the seams; it cleans well without shrinking (is usually preshrunk); and it holds its shape. If it meets these requirements, it naturally will cost more than materials which do not. Other factors which you will want to consider when you are deciding what amount you will invest in material are: how much experience have you had in making your own clothes (if you are a beginner you will probably want to use inexpensive material); how much wear is the dress to have (if it is to be used only for a special occasion an inexpensive material may be satisfactory). In the South where the summer season is long, such washable fabrics as linen and pique are the most enduring, therefore, in the long run, probably the most inexpensive. In the North where the summer season is short, a more fragile type of material will better serve the purpose.

Then, too, if styles have not drastically changed, the same foundation pattern may very easily be used for both summer and winter. You will be surprised how different the same style will look in different materials. On page 76 are four dresses designed for either summer or winter. The four may be made of summer fabrics for approximately fifteen dollars; or in winter materials for about twenty-two dollars. Dress 1, a dinner or dance dress, may be made of 4½ yards of plaid or plain organdy. This same dress made for fall wear may be crepe chiffon or satin, with metal or other trimmings. It will take the same yardage as the summer dress but the material will, of course, cost slightly more.

Five yards of linen (for an average size) will make dress 2 and its jacket. One yard of plaid material is enough for reveres, cuffs, bow and belt, or this same suit will be very smart in plain wool or plaid, or wool and taffeta, or canton and satin.

Dress 3 is of shirtmaker striped linen, pique, gingham, or the like. Four yards of material will make this sports or town-and-country dress, at least one of which should be in every woman's wardrobe. This same dress can be made effectively for fall in wool, silk, or velveteen by adding a long sleeve.

Make dress 4 (a summer suit for city or country) of cotton material, figured or embroidered, or of flowered or eyelet batiste. Without the jacket, we have a tailored frock. This same outfit is good for late summer and fall in dark sheer, with velvet belt, cuffs, and flower, or for winter in heavy crepe with contrasting jacket or light-weight wool with taffeta trimmings.

75

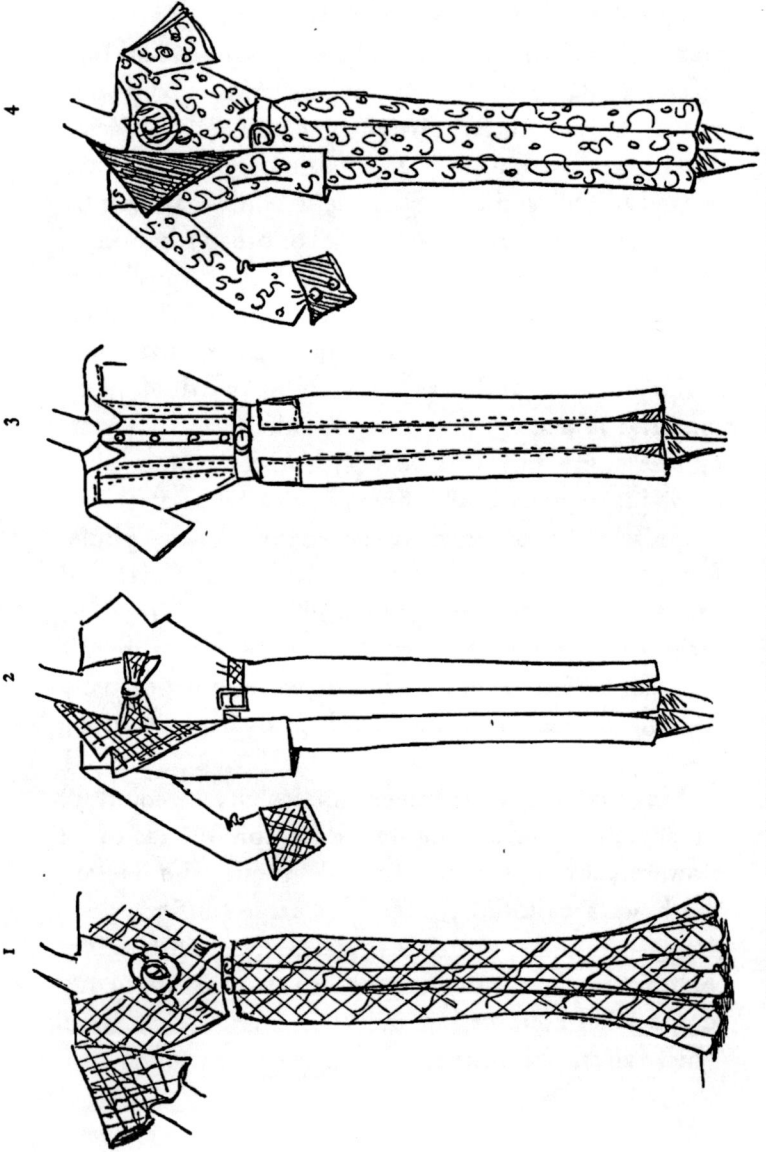

SUMMER AND WINTER WARDROBE BASED ON SAME SILHOUETTES

FINISHINGS

THE finishing touches are as important to a dress as the putting and short approach shots to a golf game. I've seen men and women who were very proud of their spectacular drive, brassie, or spoon shot but when it came to the short and most important part of the game they lacked the final touch. They failed to follow through.

Some women object to making their own clothes because they say the results look "homemade." But this certainly does not have to be the case. After the dress is put together and from all appearances finished, the "store-bought" or "homemade" stamp is yet to be placed upon it and depends entirely upon whether or not you take the trouble to follow through and add those finishing touches.

The good old-fashioned flat-iron or new electric iron helps almost as much as does the sewing machine to make your dress. In the first place the material is easier to handle if nicely pressed. And your seams, if pressed as you go along, help you to see how the dress is going to look long before it is finished. Pressing in hems, turning back folds and bias bands, give form to your creation and makes

77

it infinitely easier to add such final stitches as hand-rolling, top-stitching, and back-stitching. Always press the material on the wrong side, as pressing gives that shiny finish you do not want on the side which is to be visible.

Top-stitching is a beautiful finish for the tailored or sports dress. After the garment has been sewed together, press the seams open flat. Then on the *right* side add one or two rows of stitching on either side or both sides of the seam, a machine-foot space from it.

A *saw-tooth edge* is done on the dresses you buy to give the seam a "clean" finish. This is done with a pinking machine, but can be done at home by making notches close together with the scissors. It is so tedious a job, however, that you may find an easier solution in a small machine hem on the under seam.

French-piping is a good finish for neck and sleeves and oftentimes on the bottom of a flared skirt. Take a bias piece of material an inch wide, fold in the middle, and press so as to have a strip of double thickness. Place this strip upon the seam to be finished so that the *two* raw edges of the strip lie along the raw edge to be bound. Stitch as close to the edge as possible; turn the bias band and sew by hand on the other side (turning in the other raw edge). You now have a "clean" finish on both right and wrong sides.

78

FINISHINGS

Facing is made in the same way but is usually wider and accomplished with a single rather than a double strip.

Bound button-holes are also made with bias folds. For a one-inch button-hole cut a slit in your dress a fraction less than one inch long. Stitch the bias fold alone each side of the hole, and on the right side of the material. Pull the folds through to the wrong side and sew them down either by hand or machine.

Hand-rolling is used effectively on chiffons, organdies, and other soft materials. The edge which is to be rolled is evenly trimmed. Stitch one row by machine as close to the edge as possible. Cut off the raw selvage, dampen your thumb and index finger and roll the edge, overcasting as you go. This gives a soft finish, the finish used on handmade handkerchiefs.

The hem-line is the last finishing touch. A four-inch hem adds enough weight to make the skirt hang firmly and softly. When bottom edge of the skirt is even have someone measure and turn back the hem an even distance from the floor with tape-line or ruler, the material marked with chalk at the point where it is to be turned under.

There are two ways of finishing the under side. If a narrow hem is used, it should be pressed flat and slip-stitched to the skirt by hand. Try to keep the stitches from showing on the right side and even the hem by measuring every four or five inches.

79

Another method is to stitch seam-binding flat along the bottom edge of the skirt, turn under whatever is to be your hem allowance and finish as described with the narrow hem.

Waistline opening. Unless your dress opens down front or back there is usually an opening about six inches long under the left arm. This opening is made in the seam three inches above and three inches below the waistline. A half-inch bias band sewed completely around the opening gives it a clean finish. Either snaps or hooks are used for fastening.

If *eyelets* are to be used for a lacing effect, punch a hole in the material with pointed pencil or stiletto, and finish the edges with an old-fashioned button-hole stitch.

So with the finish of our dress, we finish also our "manual" of design.

One sunny Easter morning, in the choir row of the Episcopal church at home, my age being seventeen, I suddenly paused, completely possessed for that moment with the thrill of the appearance of Miss Agatha Pearsall walking down the center aisle, wearing my first original model!

Today I sat in our New York show room, buyers from all parts of the country viewing the "Vanity Fair" parade of blond and brunette mannikins, displaying eighty of my this-season styles.

80

FINISHINGS

In twelve years I have designed from fifteen to twenty dresses a week, approximately one thousand and forty a year, twelve thousand five hundred to date. So am I weary of seeking new combinations of color, line, and charm? Would I trade my job for any other? "Not for all the rice in China!"

May some small suggestion within these covers bring the joy of "design" to you.—For the joy is there. I believe you will find it!

OTHER LEISURE LEAGUE TITLES

The Leisure League of America is non-profit making, and is thus able to offer authoritative and entertaining hobby material at barely the cost of writing, printing and distribution. New books are appearing regularly so inquire for additional titles from your bookseller after this date.

NOVEMBER 1934

LEISURE LEAGUE OF AMERICA
30 ROCKEFELLER PLAZA
NEW YORK, N. Y.

CPSIA information can be obtained at www.ICGtesting.com
Printed in the USA
BVOW04s1203231013

334476BV00012B/635/P